Coming to Terms with Divorce

*A Guided Support Program for
Primary Grades*

Leader's Manual

by
Mary Ann Kuhn

The Center for Learning

A licensed school counselor and divorce recovery specialist, Mary Ann Kuhn is also an experienced teacher at the elementary grade level. She earned her M.A. in counseling at St. John College, Cleveland, and M.A. in family development at the University of Akron, Ohio.

The Publishing Team

Rose Schaffer, M.A., President/Chief Executive Officer
Bernadette Vetter, M.A., Vice President
Diane Podnar, M.S., Production Director
Mary Anne Kovacs, M.A., English Consultant
Lora Murphy, M.A., Social Studies Consultant

Cover Art

Robin Smith

ISBN 1-56077-147-X

Contents

Introduction

Parents, educational institutions, and social service agencies must accept the awesome challenge to meet the needs of the millions of children touched by the separation, divorce, and remarriage of their parents. The dynamics set in motion by these events are complex and need attention, support, and guidance. When left to muddle through the unending consequences of the divorce process, children risk the chance of never completing the necessary grief journey. Effects can be so long-reaching that they may affect their adult years and their own marriages.

Emerson's words, "It is not so much what is behind us or ahead of us but what lies deep inside us that matters," aptly describe the essence of healing after a crisis. Books, movies, and television provide testimonies of those who have emerged from the worst of experiences as stronger individuals. These are people who have used the grief journey to its fullest. How?

The focus of *Coming to Terms with Divorce* is to instill in children of divorce how the grief journey is accomplished:

1. To recognize that divorce is a crisis and that they need help
2. To be aware of the resiliency of youth and to build upon that quality
3. To learn what comprises the grief journey
4. To become aware that deep within themselves lies the strength that they need to walk through their journey
5. To know that they will be better persons at the end of their journey

When children live through a traumatic event such as divorce, they need support, love, tools for rebuilding, stability, and assurance that they can create a happy life for themselves.

Therefore, the following purposes define this program:

1. To create an atmosphere of love and support whereby the children of divorce can feel comfortable sharing their life stories
2. To teach the children the dynamics of divorce and its effects on them
3. To inform them of the normal reactions of children living through divorce
4. To acquaint children and their families with the many resources available in the area of divorce
5. To instill in the children their role of supporting other friends they meet in life who have experienced divorce in their families

6. To recognize that the children's workbook can provide a means of information and healing for parents as well as children

The Program Structure

The following chapters are designed to be taught in the order they are printed. Although sections could be covered independently, parts of some chapters build upon material presented in preceding chapters. Also, more difficult material is interspersed with lighter material which helps to keep the children's interest. The last chapter serves as a resource of activities that can be blended within the chapters at appropriate times.

Setting The course is designed to be taught in a school setting based on the insights of Professor Neil Kalter from the University of Michigan: "Schools nationwide are more keenly aware of the effects of divorce on children. Demand for special programs on divorce is becoming stronger as people accept that there are long-reaching effects of divorce on child development."[1]

However, the program could be adapted to counseling agencies, YWCA, YMCA, libraries or any places that can conduct a group setting.

The course could be incorporated into the school hours since its contents fall under such areas as health, citizenship, religion, and counseling. Although designed to be taught by a teacher or counselor, it is also effective if facilitated by a volunteer such as a divorced parent. In order to let the child know that there are other children facing the same challenges, a group setting is best for the course. However, a parent or relative can guide a child through the program on an individual basis.

Time allotted for the classes will differ with the setting for each group. Most schools will release the children for only thirty minutes a week. In those cases, you must decide the following:

— How to divide the chapter
— How many extra activities to include
— The length of discussion time, etc

Therefore, one chapter could take one, two, or three classes.

Other settings might allow for sessions lasting for one hour. In these cases, time could be divided in various ways. The following schedule is recommended.

— 30 to 40 minutes of workbook material
— 5 minutes break

[1] J.S. Wallerstein and S. Blakeslee, *Second Chances: Men, Women and Children a Decade After Divorce* (New York: Ticknor and Fields, 1990), 312.

— 10 to 15 minutes spent on a related item:

> Show and discuss a relevant filmstrip.
>
> Invite children to color the artwork presented and personalize the pages covered earlier in the session.
>
> Read a related story to the class.
>
> Involve children in an activity using puppets to act out scenarios relevant to the class.

— 5 minutes review of key concepts

— 5 minutes clean-up and goodbyes

The chapters leave room for you to decide what pages to cover or delete and what extra activities might be included.

Announcements

Publicity for the course, if conducted in schools, would be handled in the manner most effectively used by that particular school: school bulletin, monthly communication folder, individual flyer. A suggestion would be to send a letter home explaining the purpose of the program to

— All parents so no family would be missed

— Separated, divorced, and remarried families if such information is available and current

A sample letter is near the end of the manual.

Included in the letter should be the title of the course, facilitator, rationale, age level of participants, day, dates, time of class, location, fee for course or cost of textbook, and a phone number for further information.

A registration form should accompany this informational letter.

Other agencies/organizations could take ideas from the sample letter and use it in the manner best adapted to their purposes.

Materials

The primary material used in the workshop is the workbook itself. The course can be adequately presented by simply using the book and allowing discussion on the part of the children. They yearn to be heard and they are eager to participate.

However, a wide range of materials may enhance the program and attract children's interest. The following list provides an overview of ideas. Specific suggestions will be made in each chapter of the manual.

Crayons/markers

Art paper

Books on divorce (suggestions found in chapters)

Doll house figures

Wooden family figure sets (black and white: 2 grandparents, 2 parents and 2 children) (Childcraft, Inc.)

Puppets representing family members

Puppets of animals which are useful for expressing feelings

Dial-a-Face for identifying various moods (Ideal School Supply Co.)

Make-a-Face: hand puppets on which faces can be drawn and erased (Center for Applied Psychology)

Magazine pictures to stimulate discussion on pertinent topics

Bulletin boards which are excellent for displaying divorce concepts, copies of the children's work, etc.

Feeling Faces Paper Dolls: Find the face that fits the message you decide. This kit contains four children and two adults, each having four different facial expressions. Each doll has many shirts with feelings printed on them or blank shirts on which to write feelings. Available from   Carole Gesme
4036 Kerry Court
Minnetonka, MN 55345

Divorce Story Cards. Available from   The Center for Applied Psychology
441 N. 5th Street
Philadelphia, PA 19123

Homemade divorce puzzles (ideas found in resource chapter)

Filmstrips

Brown, L. and Brown, M. *Dinosaurs Divorce*. Filmstrip: A Guide for Changing Families, Westminister, Md.: Random House, 1986

Coping with Your Parents' Divorce. Learning Tree Filmstrips, 7108 S. Alton Way, Englewood, CO 80112, 1981. Series.

> *A Broken Home*
>
> *Must You Choose Sides*
>
> *Full Time Parent / Weekend Parent*
>
> *What if Mom / Dad Remarries*

Children in Crisis: Divorce and Separation. Parent's Magazine Films, Box 5000, 90 S. Bedford Rd., Communications Park, Mt. Kisco, NY 10549, 1975. Series.

> *When Discord Upsets the Family*
>
> *Through the Child's Eyes*
>
> *Telling the Children*
>
> *Accepting the New Lifestyle*
>
> *The Family Apart*

Equipment

Filmstrip machine
Screen

Finances

The need to charge will vary with the group sponsoring the program. Schools that incorporate it into the daily schedule or have a volunteer facilitate the group need only charge for the book. Agencies would need to follow their established fees for conducting groups. To avoid wasting class time, it is better to have the fee paid at the time of registration.

Atmosphere/ Environment

The success of this program rests on the idea that our goal is to create a support group, not a typical classroom scene, where children can explore personal ideas, feelings and concerns. A safe, relaxed, and comfortable atmosphere is vital. The room should be made pleasant—a place where the children will look forward to coming. A small portable or stationary bulletin board will allow displays on divorce.

Because of the writing, coloring, and other projects which accompany the chapters, it is important for the group to sit around a table. Round tables are most effective because they promote a closer interaction among group members.

Children like to sit on the floor. Although this is not recommended for most class sessions, it can be an option when reading a story, acting out puppet scenes, viewing filmstrips, or doing other activities of this nature.

Session Format

One or two primary goals and several auxiliary goals are listed in the objective for each session. Several key words from this paragraph could be written on a chalkboard or sheet of paper to show the children at the beginning of the class. Review and/or summary points are built into many of the children's pages throughout each chapter.

Materials

Necessary materials are listed in each chapter's manual. Enrichment materials are offered in the introduction so that creative teachers/facilitators may enhance lessons as time permits.

Preliminary Notes

Background reading and preparation time for such a class becomes a burden many teachers and facilitators cannot assume in addition to their normal responsibilities. The purpose of this section is to provide a succinct overview of the chapter material in order to enrich your background to some degree.

Recommended Books

Each chapter of the manual will list a few recommended books for the teacher which may be helpful in treating the material of that session. These suggestions have a two-fold purpose:

— To stimulate interest in specific areas

— To provide you with suggested reading material to recommend to parents requesting such resources

A more detailed annotated bibliography of books recommended for children is provided in chapter 7 of the workbook and in the Resource Materials section of this manual.

Introductory Activity

The dynamics of a support group are of the utmost importance. Although children in such a group are normally eager to share their thoughts and feelings, especially when they see how many other children are experiencing the same thing, we must still be sensitive to the child who might be inhibited. For this reason, nonthreatening openers are suggested that will help develop the group's cohesiveness from chapter to chapter.

Procedure   The procedure of each chapter consists of specific directions for each session. Although the directives are detailed, they are meant to be more of a guideline than a step-by-step procedure. Experienced teachers will present the material in their own style. Volunteer facilitators may find the steps quite helpful.

As the teacher/facilitator, you will need to consider the following:
— How much material will be covered
— How much enrichment can be added
— If a page might be done at home with a parent
— How much time can be devoted to discussion

The atmosphere and dynamics of the group must be of primary concern to the teacher/facilitator. In order to guarantee a positive learning experience, you must choose the material most beneficial to the group. The ultimate goal of the course need not be to complete every page. Unfinished pages might well be done between the parent and child in the weeks that follow the course. This is an excellent way not only to involve the parent but also to help educate him or her on the dynamics of divorce within the family.

Textbook   The workbook should be given to each child at the beginning of the course. Since the class will likely meet once a week, it might be better to collect the books after each class rather than risk their being forgotten or lost from week to week. This practice also allows the teacher a chance to make notes in the child's book. No grades should be given on this material but a positive, supportive comment on the child's paper will go a long way.

Techniques for Support Group

Formation of Groups   Since the purpose of this group is meant to be as much supportive in nature as it is educational, the size of the class is key to its success. For primary grades, four participants is ideal while more than six is ineffective. The group should be large enough for a child to see that he/she is not the only child in a divorce home, yet small enough to allow ample discussion time.

As it is likely that there will be participants from grades 1-3 in the program, several suggestions might help you when dividing these participants into groups:
1. Keeping children with their own grade level is best. To save time, it is often necessary to record answers in the first grader's books for them.

2. When there are not enough in one grade for a group, place first and second or second and third graders together.

Support Group Standards

Certain issues and ground rules should be discussed with the children prior to the class.

1. The purpose of the group: support and education

2. The distinction between this course and other school subjects:

    There are no letter grades given.

    The success of the class lies in how well they understand their family situation and feel that they can move on to a happy life of their own.

3. The importance of confidentiality: when personal stories, questions, or ideas are shared, the information must be kept within the group.

4. The nature of a support group: to help each other through difficult times; to show the members how to work through their grief journey and move on in life.

5. The atmosphere of the class is positive and pleasant in nature although the material presented and shared can be painful.

6. The child has a dual role in the group:

    — To learn as much as possible in order to help understand his or her unique family situation

    — To become aware of his/her role of reaching out to help other children whose parents are or will be divorced

Chapter 1
The Effects of Divorce

Objectives
- To introduce the concept of divorce
- To help children realize that divorce affects their lives in a broad range of ways
- To encourage children to talk about their hurts and fears
- To provide an opportunity for children of divorce to become acquainted with each other

Materials

Workbook pages for chapter 1
Crayons or markers

Notes to the Teacher

One may wonder why divorce has such a profound impact on children. Yet, we have only to reflect on the multiple changes it initiates in a child's life to catch a glimmer of such effects.

Children this age are just beginning to move out of a rather simple view of life in which they feel that everything focuses around them. They want love, security, and as many pleasures as life can offer them.

Then comes divorce which creates frightening love wars, insecurity in the realm of family life, financial status, and future plans. Mom and Dad may be sad or angry. Their lives may become a raging war over who gets what—from the house to heirlooms, the car, pets, and kids.

The term *crisis* implies that something in one's life is out-of-control, and divorce exemplifies this state at its ultimate. This results in much confusion for the child. How do children resolve the effects of divorce when they

- don't understand what is happening,
- have little control over family events,
- recognize that Mom and Dad are struggling for their own mental, emotional, and physical well-being,
- are often left out of the mainstream of activity and information?

It is imperative that significant adults in the child's life do not think that withholding information from children will automatically protect them.

Children at this age are like little sponges eager to soak in their world. They are also masters at fantasizing. Therefore, it is necessary that they be informed (to their level of comprehension) of the situation and issues at hand. Only then, with support, understanding, and guidance can they begin building a new experience in their family lives.

These sessions provide an opportunity for children of divorce to become acquainted with each other. Creating a free, honest, supportive atmosphere is an important aspect of these sessions.

Recommended Books for Teachers

Bebensee, B. *Loss—A Natural Part of Living.* Englewood, California: Educational Consulting Associates, 1980.

Berger, S. *Divorce without Victims: Helping Children through Divorce with a Minimum of Pain and Trauma.* Boston: Houghton Mifflin, 1983.

Goldstein, S. and Solnit, A. J. *Divorce and Your Child: Practical Suggestions for Parents.* New Haven, Connecticut: Yale Univ. Press, 1984.

Kurdek, L.A., ed. *Children and Divorce.* San Francisco: Jossey-Boss, 1983.

Wallerstein, J.S. and Blakeslee, Sandra. *Second Chances: Men, Women and Children a Decade After Divorce. Who Wins, Who Loses and Why.* New York: Ticknor and Fields, 1990.

Wallerstein, J.S. and Kelly, J.B. *Surviving the Breakup: How Children and Parents Cope with Divorce.* New York: Basic Books, 1980.

Introductory Activity

Since members of this class might represent children from different grade levels, ask the children to introduce themselves. Give examples of what they might say:

Name	Where they live
Grade	Who they live with
Teacher	Their favorite thing to do
Brother	What they like best at school
Sister	

Introduce yourself first and then begin with the first volunteer.

Procedure

1. Start this session by explaining that every child in the group shares something in common: their parents have been separated or divorced at least once. Break the ice by asking related questions:

   — Have you ever belonged to a group where everyone came from a divorced family?

   — Did you know there were classes like this?

   — What do you think about a divorce class?

   Allow as many minutes of discussion as it takes to get the children to begin to blend.

   Distribute the workbook to each child. Have names already printed on the cover. Let the children glance through the pages to see the chapters and pictures. Briefly explain that this book is different from any other textbook:

   — The chapters deal with many of the questions and concerns they might have about divorce.

— They are to use the book as a *guide*, then make it their own life story as much as possible.

— There are no right or wrong answers to most questions.

— There are no grades given. (If they feel better about themselves and the divorce, then the course was a success).

2. Launch the course by having the children turn to the first page of the chapter. Provide them with a red marker or crayon. Explain that this page will help them to learn quickly how they feel about themselves after living through separation or divorce. Instruct them that

if they feel very strongly their answer is *no*, circle 1.

if they feel very strongly their answer is *yes*, circle 4.

if they feel their answer is *not really*, circle 2.

if they feel their answer is *kind of*, circle 3.

Read each question aloud and give a few seconds for the children to circle the correct number.

3. Turn to page 4. The purpose of this page is to help the child distinguish between separation and divorce. Few can do this. Read the opening paragraphs to the class. Have them fill in their answer to the question, "Where did your Mom or Dad move?"

Develop the concept of divorce and have the children compare the two words. Next, have them complete the two sections comparing life before and after the separation/divorce. Spend some time sharing their answers so the children can come to see that there are both similarities and differences in responses.

4. Turn to page 6. The purpose here is to focus briefly on the topic of feelings. Many children have not come to realize their feelings adequately, much less shared these feelings with family and friends, etc.

Tell the children to choose their respective picture and draw in the facial expression that best illustrates how they felt before and after the separation/divorce and to write in the word(s) that describe this feeling. Take a few minutes to share their pictures.

Now, read the section on "What Do I Do with All These Feelings?" Instruct students to underline in color any of the items that they do with their feelings.

5. Turn to page 8. Many children have strong feelings related to how they did or did not learn about the separation/divorce. For children whose parents did not fight verbally, it might have come as quite a shock. Other children might have dreaded the divorce for years. The purpose of this page is to help children realize that it is very normal

to have a wide range of reactions to hearing the news. Those who reacted silently might be led to see that it is OK to get some of their feelings out. Those who screamed and ran down the street might learn why they reacted so strongly, for often they feel guilty or frightened about their actions later on.

6. Turn to page 10. There are sufficient directions on this page for the children. The purpose is to give children permission to acknowledge that they have been affected by the divorce whether others are aware of it or not.

7. Turn to page 11. Often children feel burdened as they carry problems around locked up inside them. Simply learning that every family has problems can help them feel better. The purpose of this page is to enable the children to focus on what seems to bother them the most at this point. This knowledge can also help a parent talk with a child about what is worrying him/her. Sharing the worry in itself can help to alleviate the burden.

Some children prefer to do this page on their own while others need your guidance. Time should be given at the end of the class to share any parts the children choose.

Chapter 2
My Journey through Loss

Objectives
- To help children realize that the grief process is normal and healthy
- To explore the stages of the grief process
- To help children realize that they can make it through the grief journey and become healthy again

Materials

Workbook pages for chapter 2
Crayons and markers
Pictures from magazines that illustrate loss:
    flowers that die
    a sun that sets
    storms that damage

Notes to the Teacher

The purpose of this chapter is to educate children and their parents in the area of grief. In order to alleviate much of the pain connected to a journey through loss, children and parents need to be informed about what to expect.

The grief process is indeed one of the most traumatic experiences in life. Every human being travels this journey sometime; yet, few are prepared for it. This, in itself, adds enormous stress on the person in grief.

People do not understand that there are many stages that they must move through after a crisis, each stage having traumatic effects on their lives. Grade schools do not incorporate the grief process into their curriculums. High schools seldom have time for it. Adults simply do not know where to turn. So, after the crisis occurs, people are forced to muddle through their grief when, in fact, education should take place prior to experiencing the loss. Many misinformed or uninformed children and adults add even another burden by wrongly believing that they experienced this loss because they were bad. To them loss is a punishment; after all, society often treats it as such. If I am

    — 5 and lost my toy,

    — 10 and lost my lunch ticket

    — 15 and lost my homework

    — 20 and lost my car keys

    — 25 and lost my promotion, or

    — 30 and lost my spouse, the reactions would often be the same:

    — I must be a bad person.

    — I must punish myself mentally.

In these situations, what led up to the loss is seldom treated. Support for the loss is not always given either. So how do we handle the dilemma? Since divorce affects such a large segment of our society, and parents are pleading for support in regard to their children, we have an excellent opportunity to teach children about this journey through loss. Children are strong and resilient. They love challenges. We must capitalize on these characteristics and guide them through their "mountain climbing" adventure in the hope that this experience will plant the seed of knowledge that will carry them through life.

Recommended Books for Teachers

Bebensee, B. *Loss: A Natural Part of Living*. Englewood, N.J.: Educational Consulting Associates, 1980.

Colgrove, *How to Survive the Loss of a Love*. New York: Bantam, 1980.

Van Ornum, W. and Mordock, J. *Crisis Counseling with Children and Adolescents*. New York: Continuum, 1983.

Introductory Activity

Ask the children to think of something they have lost in their lives. Let them share their answers with the group. One of the following questions could follow their answers:

— How did they feel after losing it?

— Did anyone understand how they felt?

— Did anyone help them to get over the loss?

Procedure

1. Turn to chapter 2, "My Journey through Loss." The purpose of this chapter is to develop two key vocabulary words: *loss* and *crisis*. Have the children take turns reading aloud the page. They can color as discussion is conducted.

2. Turn to page 16. Loss can be a very difficult aspect of life. Often the hardest part of losing something is the way we feel afterward. The purpose of this page is to sensitize children to how they feel about their loss. Children can take turns reading aloud. They may choose to underline one or two points that describe how they feel.

3. Turn to page 17. The purpose of this page is to give clear examples of various degrees of loss in a child's life. Instruct students to underline the losses they have experienced. Invite the children to discuss how these losses made them feel. Also discuss how other people tried to help them live through the loss. Every child will identify with at least one example. This will help the children realize that loss happens to everyone. To emphasize the review, all children should read the points aloud together. Then ask them which one of the five points helped them the most?

4. Turn to page 19. The purpose of this page is to help the child understand the stages of the loss journey. Read the first two paragraphs aloud. Be sure the children understand that people can feel very

differently when the same thing happens to them. One week after the divorce,

— Dad can be mad.

— Mom can be sad.

— The child can feel that the divorce is really not happening.

5. Discuss "The Loss Journey—A Grief Diagram" with the children as you go over pages 20–23 in their workbooks with them. Explain that it is all right to feel mad, sad, wishful, etc. Guide them through the diagram, the different stages of their journey:

— what each stage means

— thoughts they might be thinking as they travel through each stage

— ways they might be acting in each stage

— how they feel at each stage

6. The final step in this section, page 20, is to help the children identify where they feel they are in the journey. Even though they may be feeling several stages, the feeling that is the **strongest** right now is where they are. Have the child **outline in color** the mountain that best describes them today.

7. Turn to page 24, "Packing My Bag for the Trip." The purpose of this page is to provide a visual reminder to the children that they cannot take this trip without support. As a motivation, you might have a small suitcase or overnight bag with symbolic objects (a picture of a mom or dad, a good book, a stuffed animal, a music tape, a toy telephone, a diary or journal) in it as another visual reminder.

Chapter 3
My Feelings about Divorce

Objectives

- To lead children to come in touch with their feelings and to feel comfortable in expressing them
- To explore healthy ways children can express their feelings
- To explain that children in divorce situations do not necessarily have the same feelings at the same time

Materials

Workbook pages for chapter 3
Markers/crayons
Colored stars
Dial-a-Face
Puppets

Notes to the Teacher

This chapter focuses on exploring feelings in such a way that children learn to see feelings as a help and not something to be feared. It is easy to grow up thinking that what you feel during a crisis is wrong. The world of feelings is often a delicate subject with children since there are many mysteries as to how each child will respond to the world of divorce. It is very common for adults to "think" their feelings rather than "feel" them. Parents who can express their feelings often choose to do so away from the children because they do not want to upset them. Therefore, children learn to lock their feelings inside themselves.

This, of course, is unhealthy and impossible. Extreme anger and sadness that is "bottled" will become displaced and will express itself in very negative ways. When this happens, children are often corrected for misbehaving, in the home or in the school, rather than helped.

It is imperative for adults to learn that simply not telling children about the divorce will in no way keep them from feeling badly. Children learn more from nonverbal communication than from the spoken word, but the messages received are often confused. Therefore, they become very apprehensive as they tend to fantasize about what is wrong or what might happen.

In short, these young years are wrought with a wide range of feelings which are often unattended to in the throes of the crisis. At the top of the list are such feelings as anger, guilt, and overwhelming degrees of loneliness. But there are many others that should be reflected upon during the group session.

Recommended Books for Teachers

Krebs, R. L. *It's Hard to Tell You How I Feel.* Minneapolis: Augsburn, 1981.

Introductory Activity

Create an atmosphere whereby the children can enjoy entering into their world of feelings. If a technique such as Dial-a-Face is not available, the teacher could photocopy the blank faces available in the manual and let the children illustrate the way that they feel right now. A few minutes of sharing can take place before delving into the feeling chapter.

1. Turn to page 27. Motivate the children by pretending that they can actually climb into a "Feeling Machine." Ask such questions as the following:
   1. What might it be like in such a machine?
   2. Where would you ever go?
   3. Who would you take with you?

Procedure

Let the children take a few minutes to color their machines. Since an information center is a good place to begin a trip, it seems a good place for this imaginary trip, too.

Have the children take turns reading the five points given to them at the Feeling Information Center. Elaborate on them as you see fit.

2. Turn to page 28. The purpose of this page is to help the children understand that others can know what they are feeling by their words, their manner of speech, and their actions and gestures.

   Read aloud the three main ways that people can know how you are feeling. Together with the children, give examples of each section. Keep examples simple and to the point. For example, in number 3, you, through body language, could choose to ignore one of the children (turn your back to him or her, leave his or her name out when speaking, etc.). Immediately discuss how your actions made this child feel.

3. Turn to page 30. The purpose of this page is to provide a quick and easy way to explore some new feeling words. After introducing the first two paragraphs, have the children take turns reading the feeling word **Cars** and the synonyms under the cars. Each child will then color the car that describes how she/he is feeling right now and underline a synonym which better describes those feelings.

   Taking time to write new words will help some children learn them even better. Children can take turns finding the car that matches the feeling word listed on page 31. Have them look for the one with the same letters as those given. Instruct them to fill in the missing letters. A simple review can be done by encouraging the children to read aloud, all at once, the four short lines at the bottom of the page.

4. Turn to page 32. The purpose of this page is to distinguish between healthy and unhealthy ways to express feelings. Remember, no feeling is bad, but we can choose to express our feelings in a way

that is harmful to persons, places, and things. Take turns reading aloud the first half of the page. Then let the children silently fill in the sadness chart. Take a minute to share a few of their ideas with the class.

Allow about five minutes for children to draw and color a picture that expresses something they would do to take away a lonely feeling. Encourage sharing the pictures with the rest of the class.

5. Turn to page 34. This is the most insightful page in the unit, for children have a marvelous ability to express themselves through art. Read the opening paragraphs to them. The purpose of the page is to allow the children to express both positive and negative feelings. This is not meant to be simply an "Anger Shirt." Give children sufficient time to formulate their ideas and draw them. Since many of these pictures are so significant, you might wish to photocopy them before the children color them. Color distorts the copy. These pictures serve as excellent topics of discussion throughout the course.

6. Turn to page 35. The final page in this chapter is designed to help the children face their feelings about their parents at this point in time. The idea for this page came when the author participated in a counseling workshop in which the teacher used a family to demonstrate various possible techniques. Since it was hard for the teenage boy to describe his feelings, the counselor had the boy draw Xs on the board, representing how close each member of the family constellation was to him, in his opinion.

In this book, have the children use colored stars on paper to represent the family relationships. In this way, the children can keep their pictures in order to see how their constellations can change from time to time.

Note: You can enhance any particular section of this chapter using puppets to illustrate a point.

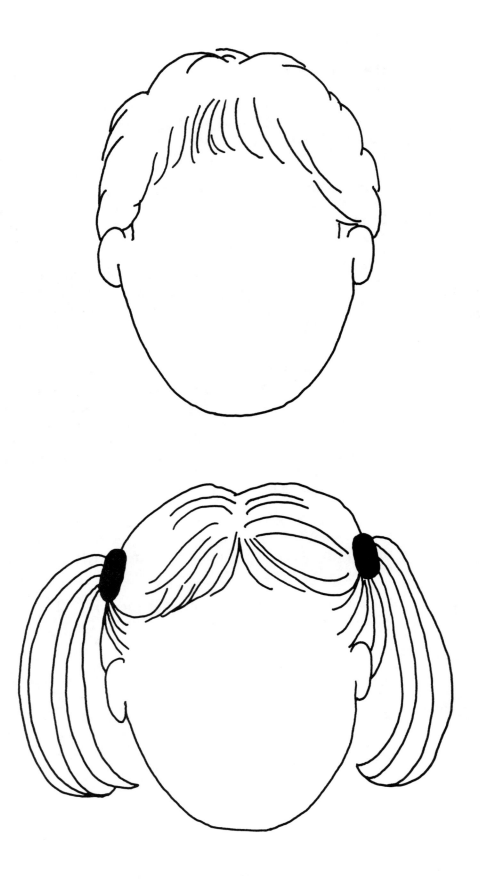

Chapter 4
My Feelings about Myself

Objectives
- To develop the concepts of positive and negative self-esteem
- To help children appreciate the uniqueness of each individual
- To enable children to see things about themselves that make them special

Materials
Workbook pages for chapter 4
Markers/crayons

Notes to the Teacher
The way children feel about themselves will strengthen or defeat them as they travel on their Loss Journey. Self-esteem is the framework on which all other aspects of the personality are built.

It has been established in previous chapters that divorce is a crisis. During a crisis, much in a person's life is usually out of control. Divorce often turns a child's world upside down. For some children, separation and divorce seem to initiate a change in every major area of life from the loss of a parent to moving which involves a change of schools and friends. These changes and the lack of order in the child's life often result in low self-esteem. This, in turn, triggers other personality characteristics that should not be ignored: extreme sadness, negative behaviors, etc.

This chapter attempts to reach out to the children whose parents are so wrapped up in their own turmoil that they devote little time and energy to helping the child sort out his or her own feelings. These pages, after being completed by the child, can help to sensitize parents and relatives to the feelings and turmoil which the child is experiencing. The child's work can also provide you with the insight as to whether the child seems able to cope with the situation or whether he or she will need some counseling along the way.

Recommended Books for Teachers
Berger, S. *Divorce without Victims: Helping Children through Divorce with a Minimum of Pain and Trauma.* Boston: Houghton Mifflin Company, 1983.

Borba, M. and Borba, C. *Self Esteem: A Classroom Affair.* Minneapolis: Winston, 1982.

Krebs, R.L. *It's Hard to Tell You How I Feel.* Minneapolis: Augsburn, 1981.

Introductory Activity
Allowing the children to begin by identifying and sharing their feelings can lead directly and effectively into the heart of this chapter. A good motivator would be to use the Dial-a-Face or the Feeling Faces Paper Dolls (listed in the Introduction section of this manual). Have the children spend a few minutes identifying and explaining their feelings.

Procedure   1. Turn to page 39. The important distinction to be made on this page is the difference between feelings towards other persons, places, and things, and the feelings one has about oneself. Feeling good about yourself can brace you for just about anything that comes your way. You may want to develop the first half of the page with the children.

Have the children take turns reading the exercise developing the concept of high self-esteem. They should underline the quote or color the picture that describes something they might have said about themselves at one time or something that someone else may have said about them at one time.

Next, have the children write at least one thing about themselves that they feel good about now: their smile, their grades, their sports, dance, or musical ability and talent, etc.

2. Turn to page 40. The key point to be developed on this page pertains to the fact that everyone has their **not-so-good** days. Having not-so-good days is normal, but how we react to them is the important issue.

Read the paragraphs at the top of the page and then lead the children in a discussion as to the various ways they have felt during such days. Take time to let the children **color** the picture that best describes their reactions to such days. Allow the children to talk about particular reactions as they color.

3. Turn to page 41. While this page appears to be strictly light in nature, it provides some excellent insights into the child's life. Watch for the answers focusing on friends. Many children cannot fill these areas in since they feel no one likes them. Whether or not a child is involved in groups and activities provides insight. A great deal of information is gained by listening to the children talk about what they wish they were involved in even though they cannot because of money or other reasons. Other points of interest on this page are phrases related to worry, wishes, goals for the future, heroes, and so forth.

Children in the third grade will want to do this page on their own, for they have a lot of fun with it. First and second graders will need help filling in their answers. If time permits, sharing this page with the class is meaningful.

4. Turn to page 42. The goal of this page is to help the children more fully understand that they are good people even when it looks like so much has gone wrong in their lives. Unless we, as teachers and other significant people in their lives, can help these children come to love themselves, they will have a difficult time loving others and receiving love later on in life.

While you can read the opening paragraph, the entire class should read the six indented lines aloud together. You will then need to help each child fill in the lines under *your self-esteem in action*.

5. Turn to page 44. The purpose of this activity page is two-fold in nature. First, children usually like activities such as connect the dots. Such a page is a timely relief after covering some heavier material. Second, this page can be one that is long remembered by the children. After they connect the dots, help the children complete the "because" section. Children easily lose sight of how special they are, especially when their lives are in turmoil.

   Allow the children time to color this page. The trophy takes on a sharp appearance when colored. If class time is at a premium, allow the children to take their books home to color all of the pictures in the first four chapters.

6. Turn to page 45. This page can be optional. However, it can, if completed, be very meaningful and leave a powerful impression on the children. Setting aside some small place in the room that could become a "Hall of Fame" for these children would be a great finale to this chapter.

   First, help the children think of neat things they do that they would love to be remembered for in a Hall of Fame: how they help at home, how they work in school, how they are kind to others, how they perform in sports, music, etc. While they are drawing their pictures, ask the children to think of things that symbolize how special they are that they could bring to class next week. This would give them an entire week to continue thinking about the message of this lesson—*self-esteem*. After they have completed their pictures, photocopy them and hang copies on the "Hall of Fame" bulletin board.

Chapter 5
Words I Need to Know

Objectives
- To inform children of the meaning of terms related to divorce
- To alleviate the fear many children have regarding these terms
- To discuss how these terms apply to their lives

Materials

Workbook pages for chapter 5
Markers/crayons
Glass's *A Divorce Dictionary*
Pictures illustrating shields

Notes to the Teacher

Once the mechanics of divorce are set in motion, many things begin to change in the home of the child. A major change is in the area of conversation. Children hear parents talking to each other, using words that actually arouse fear within them. Having a limited understanding of a word and fantasizing about the word can result in many sleepless nights.

For this reason it is vital to help children understand these words which seem to have such new found power over their lives and let them discuss how the terms are lived out in their day-to-day lives. Once the children see that lots of boys and girls have visitation rules, non-custodial parents, child support, etc., fears accumulating within them begin to lessen.

The final two pages serve to motivate the children to appreciate their own particular families—whatever the nature of these families seems to be. Such pages can provide insights into family life. Looking at the child's work, who is included in the first box, the moods of the people portrayed, the general atmosphere conveyed, is a great way of taking a peek into the pulse of the family.

Recommended Books for Teachers

Glass, S. *A Divorce Dictionary: A Book for You and Your Children.* Boston: Little, Brown & Company, 1980.

Introductory Activity

There are several simple ways to motivate the children and help create a positive attitude toward learning these challenging new words. If Glass's *A Divorce Dictionary* is available, you can take a word like *divorce,* show the picture interpretation of that word, and draw from the children what term they feel is being developed.

If Glass's dictionary, or a similar dictionary, is not available, simple pictures from magazines can be used to illustrate custodial parent (child with one parent), visitation (child with a suitcase), etc.

Procedure

1. Turn to page 49. The children can take turns reading the opening paragraphs. Next, look at the flower and show the children that the center of the flower reads *"things."* All of the other words on the flower are about things related to divorce.

    Read the words aloud so that the children can hear them pronounced correctly. The children can take turns reading each definition and filling in the letters on the correct line.

2. Turn to page 50. The most common words that children worry about are found on this page. Some common concerns are
    — "How does the judge know me?"
    — "Why are there more rules for me than for my older brothers and sisters?"
    — "Why can the court tell me who I should live with?"
    — "Why do I have to visit one of my parents when the court says I have to instead of when I want to?"

    Again pronounce the terms involved. It is best for the children to read aloud all of the definitions before beginning to match them with the words. Allow time for meaningful discussion about the terms. Many children will be able to discuss their unique courtroom, visitation, etc. stories. You should cover the final paragraph stressing its message.

3. Turn to page 51. You may want to begin by using an encyclopedia to briefly show various samples of shields. Ask the children what they think they can learn about a person, or family, just by looking at the pictures and symbols on the shield.

    It is helpful to read the page with the children, drawing their attention to the example on the bottom of the page which will help to clarify the directions.

4. Turn to page 52. As soon as the directions are clear, let the children begin their shields. Since some ideas come faster than others, the children do not need to go in order from box to box. The children might need help with their mottos. General ideas may be given to them:

Things are great	—	Things are not
Things are hard	—	Things are happier now
We are up and down	—	Life is better now

    You could photocopy the children's shields and mount and display them in the room.

    After you have copied them, allow the children to color their shields.

Chapter 6
My Special Family

Objective
- To identify the major types of families in our society
- To lead children to a deeper appreciation of their particular family lifestyle

Materials
Workbook pages for chapter 6
Markers or highlighters
Picture of different family lifestyles (optional)
A video on divorce such as "Parent Trap" (optional)

Notes to the Teacher

The primary intent of this chapter is to lead children to a deeper appreciation of their particular family lifestyle. The different types of families present in our society such as the traditional family, the extended family, the single-parent family, the adoptive family, the foster family, and the two single-parent families living together will be explored. If children can come to face their particular family situations and the characteristics and consequences of these situations, they may be able to look more positively to the future.

In an age of so much stress and confusion, family members are sometimes unable to appreciate what they have going for them. For numerous reasons many adults feel, after divorce, that they are a failure. While in this mood, it is extremely difficult for them to feel good about their single-parent home. Thus, children absorb some of the attitude of "we are a bad family," or worse yet, "we aren't a family at all."

It is imperative that we teach a clearer picture of what family life is today. Only the basic forms are developed in this primary unit. However, when the children see the variety in family life and choose the styles that describe their particular homes, some of their fears may be alleviated.

It is not the number of people within a home but the sense of belonging to the person or persons in the home that counts. As was previously developed, crisis and its inherent being-out-of-control illicits much change in the life of the divorced family. Unless the children can identify the multiple changes, it is very difficult to adjust to them. Therefore, sufficient time should be devoted to this topic.

Throughout the upheaval of the Loss Journey, coping mechanisms are developed that may be negative or destructive. When stress, anger, and untold pressures become interwoven in the lives of family members, inappropriate behaviors begin to develop known as "games." Such games, which can be described as coping mechanisms, can play havoc on family life when played by parents and children simultaneously. Yet, awareness of these games can help to change one's behavior to a healthier form of family dynamics, or at least this awareness may lead families to counseling.

Another key issue to be discussed with the children is the various challenges involved in living out family life in two places. This is no easy feat. Seldom do significant adults in their lives sit down and teach the little ones how to handle two lifestyles. At best, it is challenging. Frequently, the lessons and values learned in one home may undo the good done in another home. Purposely or not, this inhibits stability in the life of the child.

Recommended Books for Teachers

Boechmann, C. *Surviving Your Parents' Divorce*. New York: Watts, 1980.

Brogan, J. and Maiden, U. *The Kids' Guide to Divorce*. New York: Fawcett Crest, 1986.

Rofes, Eric. *The Kid's Book of Divorce*. New York: Random House, 1982. (Written entirely by children eleven to fourteen years old.)

Wallerstein, J., and Blakeslee, S. *Second Chances: Men, Women and Children a Decade After Divorce: Who Wins, Who Loses—and Why*. New York: Ticknor and Fields, 1990.

Introductory Activity

The motivation for a chapter on different family lifestyles is limited only by time. An entire class could be devoted to preparing for the content material. The following are some suggested activities.

1. A simple display of family pictures provides an excellent introduction to the concepts in this lesson. Children can describe the lifestyle they feel is portrayed and identify with those illustrations to which they feel most aligned. The children could even bring to class examples of family lifestyles which they have found in magazines.

2. Showing a video would be most appropriate at this point. The public libraries have several listings under the headings *separation, divorce,* and *remarriage.* One super example is "Parent Trap." (This film is rather lengthy.) A discussion would naturally follow such a film.

3. If audiovisual materials are unavailable, simply reading a recommended book from the bibliography to the class can be enough to capture the children's attention. This can set the tone for the lesson and also lead into the more detailed chapter 7 which introduces children to many wonderful stories about the world of divorce.

Procedure

1. Turn to pages 55, 56, and 57. Ask volunteers to take turns reading aloud the descriptions of each lifestyle. Invite the children to *highlight* the description and color the picture that go along with their particular family situation.

2. Turn to page 58. This page provides a quick way of reviewing possible changes occurring in each child's family. Read the directions slowly and allow the class to complete each direction before moving on to the next. After completing the page, have the class compare their chains. It is important to emphasize that each chain is different and that no chain is good or bad in itself, but it is how each family faces the changes in their life that counts. Again, the completed page can give insight to a parent or counselor.

3. Turn to pages 59 and 60. In separated, divorced, and remarried homes, it seems that so many things can happen on an almost daily basis to add stress and complications to interpersonal relationships. Each member of the family is walking his or her own grief journey. Often feelings seem to take over rational thinking and without fully realizing what is transpiring, one or all members of the family can be caught in the dynamics of game playing.

   Introduce the opening paragraph. Ask volunteers to read aloud each example of the games children play. Have the children *highlight* the one(s) that describes their behavior.

4. Read aloud How to Stop Playing These Games. This section explores the consequences of all of these games on each child's family dynamics. Discussion can be conducted as long as time permits for children are usually quick to cite personal examples in this area.

5. Turn to page 61. Follow the directions on the page. This page lends itself well to discussion by drawing from the class what makes this illustration of a home so unusual. This can easily lead into the many unique situations the children face in their lives. There are often several children whose other parent is totally out of the child's life. They might not see the value of this lesson. Often such children spend a lot of time at a relative's home where much of the material presented could be applied. If not, it is still important that they sensitize themselves to what their friends who do live in two places are experiencing.

   Ask each child to *outline or highlight* the phrases that pertain to them. Rather than coloring the entire picture, the house could be outlined so as not to detract from the phrases highlighted.

Chapter 7
Divorce and the School

Objectives
- To alert children to the effects of divorce that can inhibit their schoolwork
- To acquaint children with specific ways that educational institutions can serve them in times of crisis
- To emphasize the value of books as therapy when experiencing the world of divorce
- To provide an extended annotated bibliography for children and parents

Materials
Workbook pages for chapter 7
Markers or crayons
Book Loan from Public Library based on annotated bibliography found in this chapter
Specific Book:
Boegehold, B. *Daddy Doesn't Live Here Anymore: A Book about Divorce.* New York: Golden Press, 1985.

Notes to the Teacher

Divorce can have negative and long-lasting effects on the lives of children. The area of schoolwork can be particularly inhibited by the effects of divorce. It is imperative that children become aware of and understand the negative effects that crisis situations can have on schoolwork. Various forms of intervention can be introduced which can modify or alleviate these negative effects.

Many adults become absorbed and lost in their grief and feelings of loss while going through a separation or divorce. Since they can be muddling their own way through, this in turn further complicates the child's loss journey.

Getting the information of this chapter to the parents can be an excellent back-door approach to getting professional help for the parents as well as the child. They will be able to see, in a few pages, how the school life of their child can be adversely affected by the dynamics of the divorce. Many parents who would refuse help for themselves will gladly reach out for support for their children.

The school, by its very nature, plays a significant role in helping a child through the crisis of separation and divorce.
- When a parent has left the home and the family, the teacher is always in the classroom.
- When children must often leave their homes and surroundings, school is always there.

— When things at home might be very confused, and life might seem out of order, the teacher is consistent with schedules, assignments, rules, etc.

Simply directing the child to do assignments in a certain way and to hand them in on time can help to keep the child's life in order.

Many studies have shown that the most significant people in the life of a child from a divorced home should be the child's grandparents. How wonderful this would be if it were true in the majority of cases. However, circumstances often refute this premise. Grandmas and Grandpas are often caught in the middle of the divorce, and angry parents often refuse visitation of the grandchild. Many families move far away after a divorce, severing relationships with grandparents and other relatives.

Who, then, might often be the most consistent people in the child's life? They are the child's teacher and school counselors. Many children from single-parent homes are at school eight to ten hours a day (between actual class time, day care time, sports and other extra-curricular activities, etc.) School personnel care for the child consistently, day after day, in a multitude of ways throughout a time of much transition and turmoil within the family.

Adults can often choose to turn to professional help in time of crisis. Children, on the other hand, are usually unable to make such choices. Yet, within the school, there are people the children can rely upon for love and support. This chapter also provides a bibliography of books for both parents and children. Children should be guided to see books as resources that can help them get through the crises of divorce.

Recommended Books for Parents, Teachers, and Children

The annotated bibliography in this chapter introduces diverse topics about divorce covered in preschool through primary grade level books.

Recommended for Parents and Teachers
Bernstein, E., and Rudman, M. *Books To Help Children Cope with Separation and Loss: An Annotated Bibliography, vol. 3.* New York: R.R. Bowker, 1989.

Introductory Activity

Creating a pleasant atmosphere for the chapter on school is especially important, for the more that can be done to leave a positive lasting impression on the child, the better it will be for that child. A simple approach to this would be to take the book loan gathered from the library and set it up in an appealing way. Little stuffed animals scattered near the books add a special touch for this age level. Let the children take a few minutes to look through the books. Show them the one that you will read to them later on in the lesson.

Procedure

1. Turn to pages 65 and 66. While explaining the material presented on these pages, invite your students as they underline, to talk about

how these ideas fit their lives. If your students are able, allow them to take turns reading the examples listed.

2. Turn to page 67. To stress the importance of this material, you should read the various phrases printed within the schoolhouse. When appropriate, invite the children to cite examples of how school has helped them particularly in the areas presented. The children should draw a star next to the facts that apply to them. This is a good way to make an impression on them of the positive aspects of school. In this way, parents gain an insight into this subject, also. If you have time, allow the children to outline the school and background in color. Make sure that they do not color over the printed material within the schoolhouse.

3. Turn to pages 68, 69, and 70. These pages serve as a little review of the first six chapters and add a lighter touch to the material presented. However, if there is insufficient time, you could suggest to the children that they have their parent help them with the puzzles at home. This is a good way to involve the parent(s) in the course. The completed puzzles have been printed at the end of this chapter manual.

4. Turn to page 71. It is important to set the stage for the lesson on books and divorce and to develop the role of books in helping children to get through difficult times in their lives. Books have a healing power. Take time to stress the eight ways, listed on the book, that books can help people.

    Next, show the children how to make a story more fun and more effective by suggesting that they try the following: Pretend that they are one of the characters of the book. Try to feel the way that that character feels. Learn a lesson from the story that can be remembered.

    The most effective way to do this is to take a story the children have had in school and are familiar with and then apply these three steps to that story.

5. Turn to pages 72–76. Explain to the children that these pages are really for their parents so that they can learn all about the special stories written about children and divorce. You can have the children **star** the titles of the books that you feel are best for your class. Certain stories apply to particular children and this is a good way to help parents searching for appropriate help.

    At this time the children should be able to look through the book loan. Seeing the covers and the pictures of the different boys and girls in the stories seems to make them feel better. This also helps them decide which books they might like to borrow from the library.

Now, let the children choose a stuffed animal and a comfortable place to sit (perhaps in a circle on the floor).

Read them one of the books from the book loan. We suggest reading *Daddy Doesn't Live Here Anymore,* since it can be read in less than ten minutes, and the pictures are large and can be shared in a group. This book also incorporates and explores much of the message taught thus far in the workshop.

Completed Puzzles

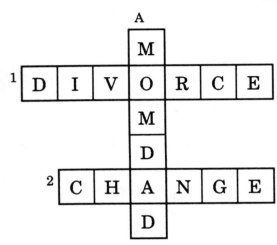

Chapter 1
Across:
1. The ending of a marriage between Mom and Dad.
2. With a divorce, lots of new things begin to happen in our lives.

Down:
A. Divorce takes place between _____ and _____.

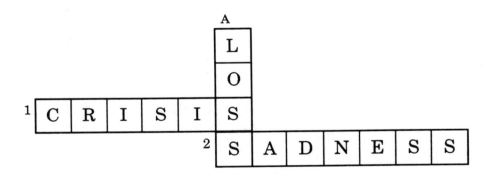

Chapter 2
Across:
1. A very big problem that is too hard to solve alone.
2. A feeling that we have for a long time after the divorce.

Down
A. The mountain climbing experience I must go through after the divorce is called my "_____ Journey."

Chapter 3

Across:

1. A feeling that means the same as "bubbly" or "excited."
2. The feeling that shows you care and feel close to another person.

Down

A. To feel weak and not able to do something.
B. To feel sad or down-in-the dumps.

```
     A
  1  H  A  P  P  Y
     E              B
  2  L  O  V  I  N  G
     P              L
     L              O
     E              O
     S              M
     S              Y
```

Chapter 4

Across:

1. The way you feel about yourself is called your _____-esteem.
2. A day when you feel "high" and things are going your way can be called an _____ day.
3. A "down" day when lots of things seem to go wrong can be called one of your _____ days.

Down

A. There is no one else on earth just like you. That makes you a very _____ child.

```
              A
        1  S  E  L  F
        2  U  P
              E
              C
              I
              A
        3  L  O  W
```

Chapter 5

Across:
1. The place where your Mom, Dad, and their lawyers meet the judge about the divorce.
2. The person trained in law to help your Mom and Dad with their divorce.

Down
A. The money given to the custodial parent to help pay for the needs of the children is called _____ support.
B. Any child under the age of 18 is called a _____.

A ... B

1	C	O	U	R	T	R	O	O	M
	H								I
	I								N
2	L	A	W	Y	E	R			O
	D								R

Chapter 6

Across
1. The name of the parent who the child lives with most of the time.

Down:
A. The whole chain of events that begins to happen after a divorce is called _____.
B. A game played by Mom and Dad where both try to pull the child to their side.
C. Lots of games are played by children in order to try to get their Mom or Dad to _____ them better.

A ... B

1	C	U	S	T	O	D	I	A	L
	H			U					I
	A			G					K
	N			O					E
	G			F					
	E			W					
				A					
				R					

Chapter 8
Little Tugs-of-War Inside Me

Objectives
- To introduce children to the push and pull effect which result from their internal and external struggles
- To help children explore both positive and negative means of coping with a crisis
- To provide practical examples that can be used to achieve a balanced outlook on life

Materials
Workbook pages for chapter 8
Markers/crayons
Bulletin board or display based on the block used to build walls
Filmstrip: "Must You Choose Sides?" (Learning Tree Filmstrips, 1981)
Suggested Book to Read: Hazen B. *Two Homes to Live In: A Child's-Eye View of Divorce.* New York: Human Sciences Press, 1978.
Puppets, dolls, paper dolls, etc. that could be used to act our internal and external struggles

Notes to the Teacher

Based on the premise that each child is unique, we know that the grief journey that they travel is just as unique. Therefore, parents, teachers, and other significant adults in their lives must be keenly alert to the external and internal struggles that children are trying to balance. Trying to deal with these struggles creates great confusion for children. Just letting them know that we are aware of their tug-of-wars and care about their turmoil is a tremendous support to them.

As we have stressed, each child is unique. Some children, then, are able to show their confusion while others bury it deeply. Some reach out for help while others close up tightly. Some children can move steadily through the healing process while others experience repeated setbacks. We must know this and act accordingly. What happens to the child who reaches out to do something caring toward a parent on the very day that the parent feels deep anger or depression and just wishes to be closed off from the world? Such setbacks often accumulate in the child's life. When these setbacks are unattended to, they can create emotional battleground within the child, leaving the child feeling vulnerable, confused, and insecure. We are called to respond to their need. We need to show them how to channel their inner struggles.

Recommended Books and Articles for Teachers

Nochols, W.C. *Therapeutic Needs of Children in Family System Reorganization: Journal of Divorce.* Summer 1984, 23-41.
Wallerstein, J. *Surviving the Breakup: How Children and Parents Cope with Divorce.* New York: Basic Books, 1980.

Introductory Activity

Visual aids help children to grasp the meaning of certain messages. The wall theme of this chapter can be visualized effectively. One suggestion is to fill paper grocery bags with crushed newspapers, leaves, etc., and tape or staple them shut. Then, have the children pile them up on their desks, in front of their faces, so that they cannot see or reach any other student. You can even write key words (fear, sadness, denial, etc.) on the bags. This way, the children can actually see that they are blocked from seeing or communicating with the other members of the support group. One by one, little by little, invite the students to remove the "stones." Now, they will realize how much more easily they can reach out and touch someone else.

Procedure

1. Turn to page 79. You could either read or call upon a child to read the opening paragraph. Have children take turns reading the things swirling around in the child's mind. There is space where children may add one or two things that they worry about a lot. A few words written by children on such exercises can allow adults to take a peek into their minds and hearts.

2. Turn to page 80. Introduce the idea of blocks by discussing the first paragraph. Then study the picture of the children behind a wall. Next, have the students color the blocks that pertain to them. The coloring must be done in a light color so that the words will not be hidden. Also, help the children fill in any other "blocks" that they might choose to write. Have the class read the "Remember" section aloud together, if reading ability allows. Otherwise, make sure to read its important messages to them.

3. Turn to page 82. This page is self-explanatory. You could read the problems in capital letters, and then invite the children to describe each problem in their own words. Guide the children in marking what they see as their problems(s). A few minutes could be spent brainstorming about other problems not listed. This would help children to choose a problem more personal to their particular situations.

   Again, read aloud the summary section on the next page. To guarantee the children's comprehension of this important material, have them take turns very briefly explaining the four points listed.

4. Turn to page 84. Since the emotional struggles of the past few pages can weigh heavily on the children, it is time to make the transition to a lighter form of learning. Thinking about ways to feel closer toward Mom or Dad does make some children feel much better. Help them understand that they can help Mom and Dad get through their grief journeys. Sometimes children do loving things but either forget their kindnesses or simply do not recognize the good that they are doing.

   The blocks describing how they treat Mom or Dad will make them aware of some of the nice things that they are doing. The children should then be led to think of other unique things that they do that bring them closer to Mom or Dad. They might need help in printing their ideas in the small sections of the balloon.

If time allows, this page colored can leave a happy impression with the children.

5. Turn to page 85. Read and emphasize the message found in the opening paragraph. An example should be given to illustrate how children choose to be happy or not. For example, if a teacher brought in candy for a class, the reactions of the children would vary. One might immediately say, "Thank you!" with a smile, while another may scowl and say; "I hate this kind!"

So, we choose to react the way we want. It is not the candy itself that makes the children happy.

The children can take turns reading the three steps of the directions. They will respond quickly with their own choices. The younger children, however, will need help in printing their answers.

The brief summary at the end of the page should be read at the end of the lesson.

Chapter 9
Starting Over Again

Objectives
- To evaluate the children's progress by having them again complete the opening questionnaire
- To pinpoint the most up-to-date problem for each child
- To develop the many options of support for the children and to let them reflect on who they feel is best able to help them with their problems
- To show children that goal setting is an easy way to take charge of life

Materials
Workbook pages for Chapter 9
Marker/crayons
Choose any extra projectile instruments which you feel are valuable
Filmstrip: Brown, L., and Brown, M. *Dinosaurs Divorce Filmstrip: A Guide for Changing Families*. Westminster, Md.: Random House, 1986.
A little snack or treat for the end of the course

Notes to the Teacher
Throughout the past eight chapters, children have been led to see that loss is a natural part of life, that being in crisis does not mean that one is bad, and that there are people who want to help them as they move through their grief journey. No course, however, is adequate in helping a person deal with a life crisis. Recovery is a process, and the process takes a long time. It is hoped that enough information has been imparted to the children that they are more aware of what divorce is, how it has affected them, and what they must do to move on in life to become themselves again!

Resparking people's lives is not an easy feat. For this reason, a simple formula for goal setting has been designed to show children that they can create a simple and direct goal in any area of their lives. Normally, goals are very general, unrealistic, and therefore quite self-defeating. People often do not like goals because they feel like failures at the end when they have not accomplished their aim.

Make sure, then, that the goals that the children set are
1. Realistic: a goal that is achievable and helpful to the child
2. Specific: one small aspect of a larger category
3. Measurable: limited so that the child can measure the success of the goal

Rather than letting the children feel that they are failures if they do not accomplish their goals, they should be taught that either their goals were not appropriate for them, or that their goals need to be adapted somewhat to better meet their needs. Remind them that people are always in charge of goals, goals are not in charge of people.

This chapter should give the children several tools for resparking their lives. It should also help them to see how much they have grown since the first class. Comparing their simple questionnaire illustrates this. The word find gives them some fun time to recognize material they have learned.

Recommended Book for Teachers

Brown, L., and Brown, M. *Dinosaurs Divorce: A Guide for Changing Families* Boston: Little, Brown & Co., 1986.

Introductory Activity

A wonderful way to create a special atmosphere for the beginning of this last chapter is to have the children enjoy the filmstrip, *Dinosaurs Divorce*. This book touches base with much of the material covered throughout the children's book. It is a pleasant, colorful, and entertaining way to review key issues. The filmstrip takes about twelve minutes, but it is time well spent.

If the filmstrip is not available through the public library, you could read a short book to the children.

Following the filmstrip or book, have the children return to page one and retake the questionnaire. This time they should use blue marker or crayon. In this way, those reviewing the questionnaire can see the change in the answers. This is a simple tool for observing growth since the first class.

Procedure

1. Turn to page 89. The purpose of this page is to lead the children to people who can help them through their grief journey. The class should take turns reading the first few words on the page. Launch the second half of the page by having the children study the picture of the scene. Draw from them their views of what they feel the picture means. Then, lead them to follow the directions at the bottom.

   The children can share their colored pictures when they are finished. Each picture might be different. Draw from the children why this happens.

2. Turn to page 90. Read aloud the first two paragraphs. Then spend a few minutes helping the children formulate what they see as their two biggest problems related to the divorce.

   The picture at the bottom is meant to emphasize the idea that we need to **reach out** in order to get help. Hiding in your room or refusing to mix with people normally results in loneliness and feelings of alienation. This is not a healthy way to handle crisis.

   There is room around the illustration to write in any particular name that is unique to the child. Hopefully this visual aid will stay with the children for years to come.

3. Turn to page 91. Direct this page carefully. Have the children refer back to the problems that they listed on page 90. Go step by step through each person(s) listed in the boxes. Instruct children to write the name of the person(s) who would be helpful to them in the boxes. Any other people, not yet discussed and not included on the chart, should be printed in the last box.

Almost without fail there will be at least one name listed on the chart for each problem. This will impart an important message to the children: there is always someone nearby to help you when you need it.

4. Turn to pages 92 and 93. It is important that a positive attitude toward this section of the chapter be imparted. First. teach the formula: What? How much? When? The best way to learn this is to see multiple examples of the goal formula. Also, compare the good goals listed with poor, unrealistic goals to help teach the message.

Learning the distinction between being a *spectator* and being a *participant* can change a child's life. Very often life's chronic complainers can be found in the spectator group. Nothing is ever good enough for them; yet, they avoid working toward solving their problems. Hopefully studying the sport picture will enable the children to keep this lesson in mind.

5. Turn to page 94. The purpose of this page is to help lead each child to formulate an individual goal. To stimulate thinking, six suggestions are given. The children should take turns reading this section aloud.

Finally, guide each child in wording a goal. It takes some practice to get the idea of how to write a goal in this way. After each goal is written the children should take time to share their goals, if they feel comfortable doing so. Help them to see that they have a specific goal, one that they can achieve.

The children should read the closing paragraphs aloud.

6. Turn to page 95. While such a page can be lots of fun for the children, it is also a means of reviewing several key ideas. Second and third graders like to do this on their own. First graders, however, need your help. Use your discretion as to when to review the words, as they are found or after the page has been completed. A light crayon or magic marker can be used to highlight the words.

Resource Materials for Teachers

Contents

Explanations Regarding Optional Resources

Objectives
- To provide supplemental resources that can be used to enrich this course
- To provide material for receiving feedback from parents regarding this book

Notes to the Teacher The following pages are comprised of supplemental resources that could be used to enrich this course. These pages will aid in gaining deeper insights into each child's view of divorce and in receiving feedback from parents. Suggested audiovisual materials are also listed that could be used to enhance the chapters.

Procedure
1. Turn to pages 43 and 44. These pages contain the sample letter to parents and registration form earlier mentioned. Pages 45 and 46 have been designed as an evaluation to help you gain insight into the course's strong and weak points. Such an evaluation is invaluable in helping you to modify the course.

2. Turn to pages 47 and 48. If you will be repeating this course, it can be helpful to tally the results of the parent's questionnaire for further comparison or contrast.

3. Turn to page 49. Noting the differences in the children's pre- and post-questionnaire found on page one of the book can be quite valuable to you, participants themselves, their parent(s), and other significant people involved in the life of youngsters. This study may help you to see strong and weak areas covered in the course, as well as areas needing more attention. Inviting the youngsters to repeat the questionnaire may help you to determine if any of the youngsters could benefit from individual counseling future.

4. Turn to pages 50 and 51. Open-ended sentences are an excellent way to gain further insight into how a child is feeling about particular areas in his or her life. You should advise your group to write down the first answer that enters their minds. When the youngsters finish, you could use a simple tally procedure to determine what themes run through the sentences.

5. Turn to page 52. "Fun with Facial Expressions" is a light way to zero in on and discover a child's feelings on a particular day regarding particular issues. Some children respond much better to drawing than to written projective tests such as the open-ended sentences. This page could be done in a class setting. Expressions could even be shared in the group. The faces could be drawn in any order and some could be skipped if not appropriate.

6. Turn to page 53. For a multitude of reasons, many children seem to love rainbows and all that they stand for. This is a wonderful way to teach children a simple lesson about life.

Rainbows are made up of two basic elements: SUN + RAIN = RAINBOW

Applying this to the children's lives, you can say that

A BRIGHT SPOT IN YOUR LIFE + SHINING THROUGH A ROUGH TIME = THE CREATION OF SOMETHING BEAUTIFUL IN YOUR LIFE

You can start this lesson with something that is troubling the child. From this, lead the child to find one little bright spot in his or her life. For example:

RAIN:	"I had to move."
SUN:	"We all live together in one house."
RAINBOW:	"There are more children where I moved, so I might have some more friends."

Or you could start with the bright spot in life:

SUN:	"Mommy and Daddy and I were a family."
RAIN:	"Mommy and Daddy did lots of fighting and then got divorced."
RAINBOW:	Mommy and Daddy aren't as mad, so there isn't as much fighting now."

SUN:	"I loved Daddy a lot."
RAIN:	"Daddy moved away from me."
RAINBOW:	"I get my own special time with Daddy now."

Sometimes we have to work hard to find something "bright" in life. This is one way to help children think along this line.

7. Turn to page 54. When film projectors are available, movies on particular topics related to the material can enrich the class considerably. Many of these can be found at a public library.

8. Turn to pages 55 and 56. Since so many schools, homes, and agencies have VCR machines, a sampling of videos on divorce can also be most helpful. Although libraries have a limited number of films on each topic, they do their best to fill the public's needs through the lending library system.

9. Turn to pages 57 through 62. Although this annotated bibliography is contained in chapter 7 of the child's book, it is an excellent resource to have separate and available to give teachers and parents when they turn to you for help.

Sample Letter to Parent(s)

Dear Parent(s)

Throughout this semester a course will be offered through the school for primary grade children who live in families touched by separation, divorce, and/or remarriage.

The rationale for this course is based on a quote by Professor Neil Kalter from the University of Michigan which is found in *Second Chances: Men, Women and Children a Decade After Divorce.* by Judith Wallerstein and Sandra Blakeslee, 1990. Professor Kalter states that schools nationwide are more keenly aware of the effects of divorce on children. Demand for special programs on divorce is becoming stronger as people accept that there are long-reaching effects of divorce on child development.

Therefore, the following program is available for your child(ren) if you so choose.

A Workshop on Divorce
for
Primary Grade Children, Grades 1–3

Facilitated by _____

Conducted: Every Tuesday afternoon
2:00 - 2:30 pm
In the school library
From September 25 to January 15

Fee: For the workbook _____ and/or
For the course _____

The course will cover a wide range of information that will help children understand the process they must journey through while experiencing or having experienced separation, divorce, and/or remarriage. Some examples of the material covered are:

The Effects of Divorce	My Special Family
My Journey through Loss	Divorce and the School
My Feelings about Divorce	Little Tugs-of-War Inside Me
My Feelings about Myself	Starting Over Again
Words I Need to Know	

If you are interested in this course, please complete the attached registration form and return to me by _____ .

If you have any questions, please call me at _____ .

Thank you for your support of this program.

Registration Form
for Workshop on Divorce for Primary Grade Children

Student's Name _____ Age _____ Grade _____

Address _____

Teacher _____

Phone _____

Family Status: ❑ Separated ❑ Divorced ❑ Remarried

Any comments that you would like to include which might be helpful in working with your child:

_____

_____

_____

_____

_____

_____

_____

_____

_____

_____

_____

_____

Please include the registration and/or book fee with your registration.

Parent(s) Signature _____

Parents' Questionnaire

Dear Parent,

Would you be so kind as to complete this evaluation sheet regarding the divorce workbook that your child has completed? Your comments will help in modifying any parts that need change, thus serving the needs of your child and other children more effectively.

Evaluation

Yes   No   1. Has your child discussed the course with you?

Yes   No   2. Are you glad that such a course was offered for your child?

Yes   No   3. Did your child seem to like coming to class?

Yes   No   4. Was there any part of the course that your child seemed to especially enjoy? Please explain.

_____

_____

_____

Yes   No   5. Do you feel that your child understands divorce better than he or she did before the course?

Yes   No   6. Does your child seem more open to talking about your divorce?

Yes   No   7. Does your child appear to be more in charge of his or her life? For example, is your child not blaming others as much for his or her problems? Has your child stopped taking his or her anger out on others?

Yes   No   8. Would you say that your child has a better feeling about his or herself since the course began?

Yes   No   9. Do you feel that the course has helped your child learn how to cope with the divorce?

Yes   No   10. Do you feel that your child has a better feeling about facing the future since the course began?

Yes   No   11. Does your child feel that he or she is the only person going through the effects of divorce?

Yes   No   12. Do you have any suggestions which would help make the course
                   more effective for your family?

_____

_____

_____

_____

               13. Would you like to add any other comments?

_____

_____

_____

_____

Thank you for your cooperation and support. Please return this paper at your earliest convenience.

Tally Sheet for Parent's Questionnaire

Yes _____ No _____   1. Has your child discussed the course with you?

Additional comment: _____

Yes _____ No _____   2. Are you glad that such a course was offered?

Additional comment: _____

Yes _____ No _____   3. Did your child seem to like coming to class?

Additional comment: _____

Yes _____ No _____   4. Was there any part of the course that your child especially enjoyed?

Additional comment: _____

Yes _____ No _____   5. Do you feel that your child understands divorce better than he or she did before the course?

Additional comment: _____

Yes _____ No _____   6. Does your child seem more open to talking about your divorce?

Additional comment: _____

Yes _____ No _____   7. Does your child appear to be more in charge of his or her life?

Additional comment: _____

Yes _____ No _____   8. Would you say that your child has a better feeling about his or her self since the course began?

Additional comment: _____

Yes _____ No _____   9. Do you feel that the course has helped your child learn how to cope with the divorce?

Additional comment: _____

Yes _____ No _____   10. Do you feel that your child has a better feeling about facing the future since the course?

Additional comment: _____

Yes _____ No _____   11. Does your child feel that he or she is the only person going through the effects of divorce?

Additional comment: _____

12. Do you have any suggestions which would help make the course more effective for your family?

_____

_____

_____

_____

_____

_____

_____

_____

_____

_____

_____

_____

_____

_____

A Comparative Study Chart
for the Questionnaire on Page Three of the Workbook

	Pre-Test				Post-Test			
	No			Yes	No			Yes
	1	2	3	4	1	2	3	4

1. Do you feel that you understand what divorce is?

2. Do you think that you understand what your mom and dad have gone through?

3. Do you feel that your mom and dad understand what you are going through?

4. Do you feel that you are partly to blame for their divorce?

5. Do you have someone to talk with about your parents' divorce?

6. Do you wish that you had someone else to talk with about your parents' divorce?

7. Do you know who to turn to for help when you have a big problem?

8. Do you feel good about yourself right now?

9. Do you have the feeling that you are the only child going through the kind of divorce problems that you have?

10. Do you think that you will ever be happy again?

Open-Ended Sentences

1. I like to _____

2. I think that my family _____

3. I wish _____

4. My dad thinks that _____

5. To me, divorce _____

6. I feel lonely when _____

7. The harder I try _____

8. My mom thinks that _____

9. I want to be like _____

10. To me, books _____

11. When kids ask me if my parents are divorced, I _____

_____

12. At school, I _____

13. I worry a lot about _____

14. I know I am special because _____

15. My visitation day with Mom/Dad is _____

16. Living in two places makes me _____

17. The hardest thing about divorce is _____

18. I feel happiest when _____

19. The person who tries to help me the most is _____

_____

20. The thing I feel the angriest about is _____

21. I wish my family _____

22. I feel afraid when _____

23. When I think about money, _____

24. To me, fighting is _____

_____

25. When I think about my mom or dad remarrying, I _____

_____

26. On a "down" day, I _____

27. On an "up" day, I _____

28. My biggest dream _____

29. When I feel really, sad, I _____

30. I am best at _____

Fun with Facial Expressions

Here Is How I Feel about Some Events in My Life

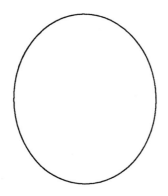

I Am Getting Ready to Visit
Mom or Dad.

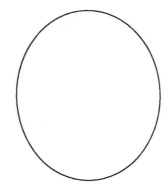

I'm on My Way to School.

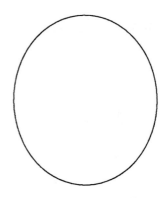

The Way I Feel about Mom or
Dad Remarrying

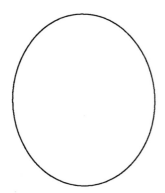

It's Time for Me to Get Up in
the Morning.

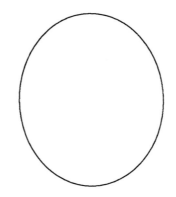

When I Think about Money
I Feel . . .

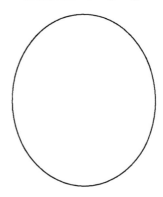

The Way I Like to Feel Most of
the Time

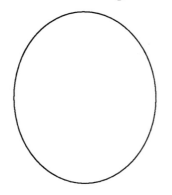

The Way I Feel about Divorce

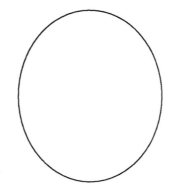

Friends Make Me Feel . . .

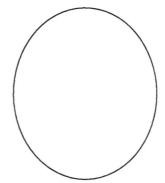

When I Go to Bed at Night I
Feel . . .

Rainbow Worksheet

| The Sun | + | Rain | = | A Rainbow |

A Bright Spot in My Life + Shining through a Rough Time = The Creation of Something Beautiful in My Life.

Suggested Films on the Topic of Divorce for Primary Grade Children

All reviews have been taken from *Educational Film And Video Locator of the Consortium of College and University Media Centers and R. R. Bowker. 4th Rd.* 2 vols. New York: R. R. Bowker, 1990-1991.

Divorce and Other Monsters. 16 mm, 22 min. 1981. Distributed by Barr Films, Irwindale, Cal.

Audience: K through intermediate

Sandy's parents have recently divorced and she is experiencing the anger, fear, guilt and rejection that many children feel after a divorce. It takes awhile, but after talking with her friends, her teacher, her mother and father, Sandy realizes that the divorce wasn't her fault.

Family in the Purple House. 16 mm, 13 min. 1970. Distributed by Phoenix/BFA Films and Video, New York.

Audience: Primary

A seven-year-old child explains the lifestyle of his fatherless home. Are families different when parents are divorced? How do children respond and grow up?

Suggested Videos on the Topic of Divorce for Primary Grade Children

All sources have been taken from Weiner, D. ed. *The Video Source Book 11th ed.* 1 vols. Detroit: Gale Research, 1990.

Divorce Can Happen to the Nicest People. Beta, VHS, 30 min. Distributed by New World Video, Los Angeles.

Audience: Primary through Junior High

An animated program designed to explain the process and motivations behind divorce.

Feeling Left Out: A Film about Divorce. Beta, VHS, 15 min. 1975. Distributed by AIMS Media, Van Nuys, Calif.

Audience: Primary to Senior High

Designed to help children through their temporary sense of isolation and depression after their parents are divorced.

First It Seemed Kinda Strange. Beta, VHS, 6 min. 1976. Distributed by Films, Inc., Chicago.

Audience: Primary

A child whose parents are divorced lives with his mother, visits his father and stepmother regularly and realizes that things are actually better since the divorce.

Hayley's Home Movie. Beta, VHS, 23 min. 1988. Distributed by AIMS Media, Van Nuys, Calif.

Audience: Family

The story of a young girl named Hayley and her reaction to her parent's separation.

Home Sweet Homes. Beta, VHS, 20 min. 1983. Distributed by Filmakers Library, New York.

Audience: Family Education

This tape interviews five children who are under joint custody of their divorced parents.

Me and Dad's New Wife. Beta, VHS, 33 min. 1976. Distributed by Time-Life Film and Video, Paramus, N.J.

Audience: Primary to Junior High

Tells the story of a twelve-year-old daughter of divorced parents who on her first day of junior high finds that her math teacher is her father's new wife.

Mom and Pop Split Up. Beta, VHS, 15 min. 1979. Distributed by Barr Films, Irwindale, Calif.

Audience: Primary to Junior High

An animated film about the problems a girl faces when her parents get divorced.

The Way It Is: After the Divorce. Beta, VHS, 24 min. 1983. Distributed by the National Film Board of Canada, New York.

Audience: Primary to Adult

Program looks at problems that occur with children caught in the middle of a divorce.

Wreck of a Marriage Series. Beta, VHS. 1988. Distributed by Centre Productions, Boulder.

Audience: Primary to Adults

This is a presentation of three animated videos which can help alleviate the feelings of confusion and guilt commonly held by children in divorced families.

When Divorce Comes. VHS, 13 min. 1987. Distributed by Film Ideas, Northbrook, IL.

Audience: Intermediate through Junior High

More than 40% of the school-aged population has parents who are either separated or divorced. In this program, young people from intermediate grades through high school openly express their anguish and pain as they talk about the break up of the family, providing a valuable tool for discussion on the impact of divorce on youth.

Fun with Books

An Annotated Bibliography for Preschool through Grade Three

Ages:

4-8   Baum, L. *One More Time*. New York: Morrow, 1986.

This little story tells about the joys and fears of Simon's visiting days with his dad. After spending a wonderful Sunday together, Simon gets anxious when it is time to say goodbye. This story is an excellent way to help parents and children open up this stressful topic for discussion.

7-10   Berger, T. *A Friend Can Help*. Chicago: Childrens Press, 1974.

In this book, a child psychologist helps an eight-year-old girl whose parents are divorced to open up and talk things out with a friend. Full page photos show the many emotions and moods which can be felt during such a crisis.

8-12   Berger, T. *How Does It Feel When Your Parents Get Divorced?* New York: J. Messner, 1977.

This story with photos grasps the dynamics of the emotions of an eight-year-old child who is experiencing divorce in her family. This very touching book discusses these problems and emotions through the eyes and heart of a young child whose lifestyle has changed significantly because of her parents' divorce.

4-8   Boegehold B. *Daddy Doesn't Live Here Anymore: A Book about Divorce*. New York: Golden Press, 1985.

Darling little Casey finds herself so sad over all of the fighting going on between her mommy and her daddy. She sees that Dad is gone more and more, and Mom is crying more and more. Finally, one day, she is told that although both Mom and Dad love Casey very much, they do not love each other and will be getting a divorce. The story unfolds showing Casey's reactions which range from crying to trying to bring them together again, to taking the blame on herself, to even trying to run away. With the love and support of her parents, Casey learns how to live her new family life.

1-3   Brown, M. *The Dead Bird*. Reading, Mass.: Addison-Wesley, 1965.

This is a touching story of several children who come upon a little bird that had recently died. Facts about death are interwoven within the plot. The children learn certain physical characteristics of death: the body stiffens, gets cold, there is no heartbeat.

The children decide to care for the dead bird just like adults do when someone dies. They decide on a funeral, dig a grave, collect plants and flowers, and show their feelings by singing a song and crying. The various stages of grief are simplistically incorporated and treated well. They experience sorrow, share grief, and look for support until finally time gradually heals their pain.

5-10   Brown, L., and Brown, M. *Dinosaurs Divorce: A Guide for Changing Families*. Boston: Little, Brown & Co., 1986.

> This delightful book is composed of marvelous illustrations portraying many of the major areas involved in divorce and family life as seen by young children. And, it is all done through clever little dinosaur characters who captivate the young readers. Profound topics such as what leads to divorce, feelings related to divorce, visitation days, celebrating holidays in two places, parents dating and remarrying, etc., are all explored. Children of all ages love this book.

3-7   Caines, J. *Daddy*. New York: Harper & Row, 1977.

> This little story emphasizes the special relationship that exists between Windy and her dad. Even though Windy gets wrinkles in her stomach during the week when she worries about her dad, they immediately disappear when he arrives early Saturday morning for their day together. The story beautifully shows that the noncustodial parent need not buy his or her way into the heart of the child.

6-8   Conta, M. and Reardon, M. *Feelings Between Kids and Parents*. Chicago: Children's Press, 1974.

> Fourteen parent/child situations are briefly presented and accompanied by a full-page colored photograph. Following the explanation of the "feeling situation," key questions are asked that may stimulate sharing between parent and child.

6-9   Dragonwagon, C. *Always, Always*. New York: Macmillan, 1984.

> Beautiful full-page pictures highlight a tender story of a young girl who learns how to treasure special memories from both her home with Mom in New York and her home with Dad in Colorado. Her parents worked very hard to show her that even though they were divorced, their love for her would go on always.

3-8   Girard, L. *At Daddy's on Saturdays*. Niles, Ill.: A. Whitman, 1987.

> Katie's mom and dad are separated and will soon be divorced. The author clearly presents to the reader all of the worries, changes, and reactions of a young child to divorce. Any parent reading this book to a child would see the importance of divorced parents respecting each other and working together for the sake of the child.

3-6   Goff, B. *Where Is Daddy?: The Story of a Divorce*. Boston: Beacon, 1969.

> This is a touching story which will help guide parents (who are themselves struggling with great pain and confusion) to take an overwhelmingly puzzling event and break it down to manageable size for their children. Through the character of little Janeydear, sensitive areas regarding divorce are treated. Such a tender story can serve as a mirror reflecting the problems common to many families.

4-8   Grollman. E. *Talking about Divorce and Separation: A Dialogue Between Parent and Child*. Boston: Beacon, 1975.

> This book is a two-part guide to helping small children of divorcing parents face the reality and consequences of family breakup. It con-

tains an illustrated children's "read along" section that can help open the door to dealing with the difficult subject of divorce for a child. It also includes sources for further help and a bibliography of fiction and nonfiction about divorce.

3-7　　　Hazen, B. *Two Homes to Live In: A Child's Eye View of Divorce.* New York: Human Sciences Press, 1978.

Niki, a young girl, explains how she comes to terms with her parents' divorce. She learns that parents, not children, divorce. She also realizes that the children are not to blame and that it is normal to have the fears and dreams which she experiences. This book deals with the idea that big adjustments have to be made as parents separate and divorce, but slowly these adjustments can be made as others offer their love and support.

8-10　　　Hurwitz, J. *DeDe Takes Charge!* New York: Morrow, 1984.

DeDe is a delightful young girl who the reader easily comes to love. She is in the middle of her divorced parents, trying to do what many children do—please both Mom and Dad. This is a challenge since Dad demands perfection while Mom is anything but perfect. Even with such different parents, DeDe knows they love her and want to take care of her, both in their own way.

5-8　　　Lisker, S. *Two Special Cards.* New York: Harcourt Brace Jovanovich, 1976.

Both the story and the large descriptive pictures do an excellent job of conveying key issues in the life of an eight-year-old child whose parents are divorcing. The greatest emphasis in the book lies in the gradual transition of living in two different places, showing that it is possible to love each parent very specially, and in turn, to be loved deeply by two separated or divorced parents.

2-4　　　Mann, P. *My Dad Lives in a Downtown Hotel.* Garden City, N.Y.: Doubleday, 1973.

The author beautifully presents the typical feelings of a young boy after his parents' divorce. For Joey, divorce means guilt, hopes for reunion, shame over not having a dad in his home, anger at his dad, and sadness for his mom. The author takes this painful situation and shows that it does not have to be the end of the world, for Joey is able to use his creativity to help find answers to his problems. Although there is some fantasy in his solutions, the book is filled with great insight into children's feelings.

7-9　　　Newfield, M. *A Book for Jodan.* New York: Atheneum, 1975.

Jodan lived her nine young years in an almost too-good-to-be-true way, sharing in so many fun activities that she and her parents did together. It was such a shock to her when these events were replaced with tension, quarrels, loud arguments, and finally separation. Jodan did not even get to see her dad since she lived in California and he lived in Massachusetts. The author sensitively and creatively presents an idea whereby a parent and child can capture precious moments to treasure during times when they are apart and lonely. A scrapbook made by both Dad and Jodan encompasses every level of human development. Indeed, just reading this book can serve as a source of many helpful ideas to parents and children alike.

6-9   Paris, L. *Mom Is Single*. Chicago: Childrens Press, 1980.

This story with full-page color photos, portrays a seven-year-old boy's feelings about his parents' divorce. The story presents many of the common experiences children learn to cope with when living with single working moms. The anger and insecurity arising from questions such as "Why did things have to change," "Could Mom leave, too," "Is Daddy lonely?", etc. are resolved through talking things out and coming to understand that just because Mom and Dad do not live together does not mean that they do not care about their child.

3-5   Perry, P. *Mommy and Daddy Are Divorced*. New York: Dial, 1978.

Joey and Ned work hard at trying to understand why Daddy and Mommy divorced. They ask questions in order to try and learn about their new way of living. Although there are times when they are sad, there are also times when they share very happy moments in their new family life.

5-8   Schuchman, J. *Two Places to Sleep*. Minneapolis: Carolrhoda, 1979.

Seven-year-old David describes what it is like living with his dad and visiting his mom on weekends. Interwoven in the story are the adjustments needed as a result of divorce. This book also explores everyday things parents and children can do to strengthen their relationship. Divorce is seen as something you do not like but cannot change. The story clearly emphasizes that the child is not the cause of the divorce.

K-2   Stein, S. *On Divorce: An Open Family Book for Parents and Children Together*. New York: Walker, 1979.

This unique presentation of a child's book on divorce can be used in a variety of ways. The format of its 47 pages is generally done in this manner. One page is a black-and-white photograph of either Becky, her parents, or her two little friends. The opposite page has 1/2 inch print telling the storyline for the child along with small print with a great deal of information for the parent. The latter analyzes the primary story and gives practical recommendations for the adult.

3-7   Stinson, K. *Mom and Dad Don't Live Together Anymore*. Toronto: Annick, 1984.

The little girl in this story teaches young and old alike about the many thoughts and worries children have about divorce. By looking at the pictures and reading about the child's concerns, the reader will learn that children can come to know that Mom and Dad love them dearly although they no longer love each other.

6-8   Thomas, I. *Eliza's Daddy*. New York: Harcourt Brace Jovanovich, 1976.

Eliza would yearn for Saturdays when her dad would visit her. They would go wherever Eliza suggested. She was a little jealous over her daddy's new family which consisted of a new wife, a stepdaughter

Eliza's age, and a baby boy. After some troubled dreams, she finally got up enough nerve to ask to visit his new home. What a pleasant time that was.

5-8   Vigna, J. *Grandma without Me*. Niles, Ill.: A. Whitman, 1984.

This story superbly treats the topic of grandparents and grandchildren being separated due to a divorce. Colorful pictures and a touching story show how a grandma and her darling little grandson remain very close even though they cannot see each other. A scrapbook holds their special moments which they will share when they can see each other again.

4-8   Vigna, J. *Mommy and Me By Ourselves Again*. Niles, Ill.: A Whitman, 1987.

The author, in a few pages, treats several major areas of stress in the life of a child from a divorced family. Amy's dad never comes to visit her and this hurts her a lot. Amy's mom was dating a man who was kind to Amy, but the romance ended and Amy lost again. Soft pictures and carefully chosen words help the reader to learn that with love and support, children can heal from such situations.

1-3   Viorst, J. *The Tenth Good Thing about Barney*. New York: Atheneum, 1971.

This classic little story about a boy's pet cat that dies helps to walk a child through the stages of loss. The little boy's mom and dad support him a lot through his time of sorrow. He is so sad he can't even eat or watch TV. Together the family plans a funeral for Barney. Dad tells his son to think of ten good things about Barney which can be told at the funeral. Through this experience, the little boy learns that life is not wasted by death, but death helps to contribute to new life.

K-3   Wilt, J. *Handling Your Ups and Downs*. Waco, Tex.: Educational Products Division World, 1979.

Handling Your Ups and Downs is a delightful book for young readers covering a wide range of emotions which children experience during their good and bad times. The author, through art and well-chosen words, explains to children what happens as they move from one emotion to another. Grief, loneliness, anger, guilt, security, and many more feelings are understood as the children are walked through simple exercises and clearly developed terms.

K-2   Zolotow, C. *My Grandson Lew*. New York: Harper and Row, 1974.

The depth and beauty of this little five-minute story is difficult to adequately describe. Zolotow masterfully teaches parents the importance of supporting their children through a grandparent's death rather than just pretending it never happened. The reader learns, through the eyes of a little boy, just how many treasured memories children have from their early years. And when these memories are about a deceased grandparent, how much better it is to be able to share these with your parent rather than both parent and child suffering alone and silently.

K-3   Zolotow, C. *The Quarreling Book.* New York: Harper and Row, 1963.

When Mr. James started the day by forgetting to kiss his wife good-bye one morning, a bad mood started in the family that ended up spreading all the way to the children's school. This short little story lets children learn that a simple little thing can turn a big, bad mood around in a family. Since many families experiencing loss have lots of bad moods to handle, the story is excellent for use as an opener for any group session with children. It will never be outdated.

THE PUBLISHER

All instructional materials identified by the TAP® (Teachers/Authors/Publishers) trademark are developed by a national network of teachers whose collective educational experience distinguishes the publishing objective of The Center for Learning, a non-profit educational corporation founded in 1970.

Concentrating on values-related disciplines, The Center publishes humanities and religion curriculum units for use in public and private schools and other educational settings. Approximately 300 language arts, social studies, novel/drama, life issues, and faith publications are available.

While acutely aware of the challenges and uncertain solutions to growing educational problems, The Center is committed to quality curriculum development and to the expansion of learning opportunities for all students. Publications are regularly evaluated and updated to meet the changing and diverse needs of teachers and students. Teachers may offer suggestions for development of new publications or revisions of existing titles by contacting

The Center for Learning

Administrative/Editorial Office
21590 Center Ridge Road
Rocky River, Ohio, 44116
(216) 331-1404 • FAX (216) 331-5414

For a free catalog, containing order and price information, and a descriptive listing of titles, contact

The Center for Learning

Shipping/Business Office
P.O. Box 910
Villa Maria, PA 16155
(412) 964-8083 • (800) 767-9090
FAX (412) 964-8992